Exploring Viking times

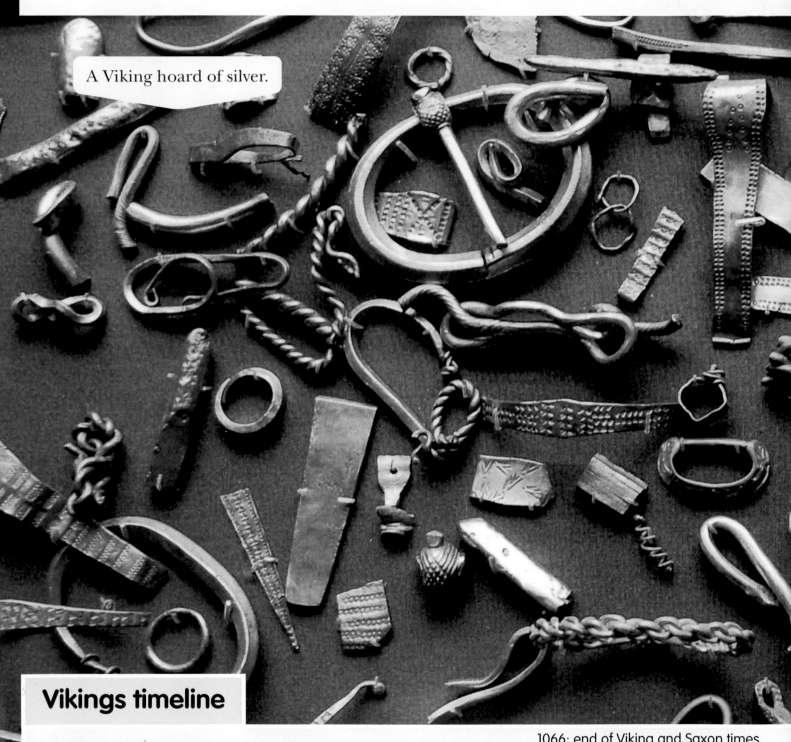

A Viking hoard of silver.

Vikings timeline

First Viking raid on Britain

The Danes Great Army invades

The Danelaw is created

Danish Viking King Sweyn becomes King of England

1066: end of Viking and Saxon times Norman William the Conqueror becomes King of England

790		890	990	1090

First Norwegian Viking raid on Scotland

First Danish Vikings stay in England

Many battles take place between the Saxons (Alfred) and Vikings

Anglo-Saxon Ethelred becomes King of England

Vikings (800–1066/1400)

0	1000 AD		2000 AD

–146BC)

Anglo-Saxons (450–1066)

Tudors (1485–1603)

Victorians (1837–1901)

Romans (700BC–476AD)

Contents

Look up the **bold** words in the glossary
on page 32 of this book.

Norwegian Vikings give all Scottish islands
except Orkney and Shetland to Scottish kings.

1472: Vikings give Orkney and
Shetland back to Scotland

1190	1290	1390	1490

Viking raids on Scottish
mainland are defeated

Meet the Vikings

The Vikings were country people from the coasts of Norway and Denmark. In winter it was cold and so they knew how to protect themselves by wearing woollen and linen clothing.

Men wore trousers and tunics and women wore long dresses. All wore leather shoes and woollen stockings.

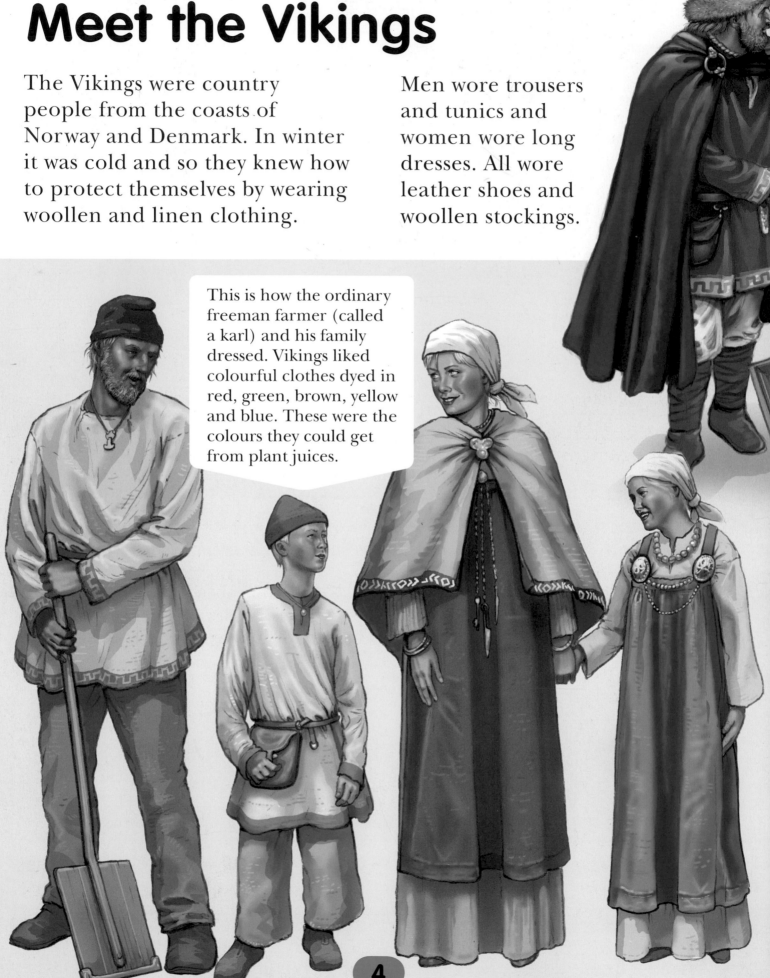

This is how the ordinary freeman farmer (called a karl) and his family dressed. Vikings liked colourful clothes dyed in red, green, brown, yellow and blue. These were the colours they could get from plant juices.

Did you know… ?

- The Vikings were one of the few ancient peoples to bathe. They all bathed once a week – on a Saturday.
- Linen is made from the fibres in a plant called flax.
- Wool was picked up from the ground as sheep moulted, then spun and woven.
- Vikings did not have coins. Viking money was the jewellery they wore. When they needed to pay someone, they chopped off a piece of silver armband and gave it to them.

Nobles and warriors dressed differently. They were more wealthy as they were the ones who collected the **booty** from raids. For battle some wore an iron helmet and chain mail, but most wore thick leather coats and helmets.

Q **What did they use to colour their clothes?**

Viking longships

The Vikings were famous for their **longships**. They used them to cross the North Sea and even to reach America.

Longships were the largest ships the Vikings had. They were also the fastest of their ships and designed for war. The large central space was for carrying **booty** back home after a raid.

They also had smaller ships of similar design for carrying cargo when they traded with other people.

The longship is a kind of galley, that is a ship with oars as well as sails. Sails were used most of the time. Oars were used near the coast because they made the ship faster and more manoeuvrable.

Did you know... ?

- There were no toilets on a Viking longship.
- Vikings had no compass and many Vikings lost their way and were never seen again.
- The Vikings put their shields on the outside of the boat to give more room inside.
- Longships could travel at about 15 km an hour.
- A longship was not large by modern standards – about 25 m from bow to stern.
- Longships were flat-bottomed boats which could travel up small rivers easily.

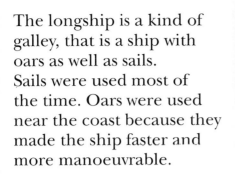

Q **When were the oars used?**

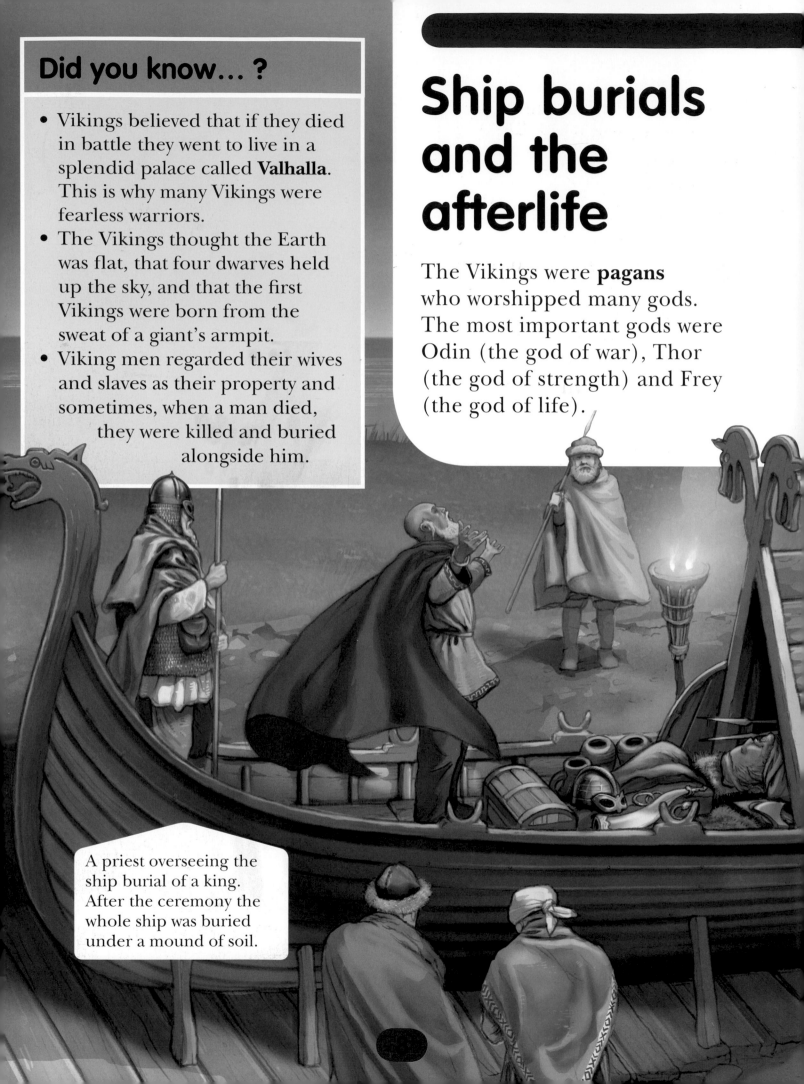

Did you know… ?

- Vikings believed that if they died in battle they went to live in a splendid palace called **Valhalla**. This is why many Vikings were fearless warriors.
- The Vikings thought the Earth was flat, that four dwarves held up the sky, and that the first Vikings were born from the sweat of a giant's armpit.
- Viking men regarded their wives and slaves as their property and sometimes, when a man died, they were killed and buried alongside him.

Ship burials and the afterlife

The Vikings were **pagans** who worshipped many gods. The most important gods were Odin (the god of war), Thor (the god of strength) and Frey (the god of life).

A priest overseeing the ship burial of a king. After the ceremony the whole ship was buried under a mound of soil.

They believed that when they died, they would go to meet these gods. To be able to hold their heads up high they would need to show that they were worthy, and so they had to take their valuables with them.

As a result, important Vikings were buried with their precious goods and sometimes they were buried in their own ships.

Did you know…?

- Viking gods were like super-humans.
- Vikings inherited their gods from the Romans and ancient Greeks.
- Odin (Woden) has given his name to Wednesday.
- Thor has given his name to Thursday.

Q What treasures do you think might have been buried with the king?

Sagas

The Vikings did not write their stories down, but passed them on by word of mouth from one generation to another. These stories told of great bravery and wicked treachery. They were called **sagas** and were told around the fires in the Viking **longhouse** to while away the long winter evenings.

Some sagas were short and told of the way that the adventures of boys turned them into men. Others were very long and rather like violent fairy tales.

Q **Can you make up a story (saga) to go with this picture?**

This is the kind of thing a saga would include: a story about how a fearsome beast was tracked down and slaughtered.

Did you know... ?

- The Norwegian Vikings wrote almost nothing down. The sagas were written in Iceland, centuries after they were first told, and may be very inaccurate.
- Viking writing was made up of short, straight strokes, called **runes**.

Vikings raid a monastery on the eastern shore of England.

The Vikings in England

The first time anyone in England saw the Vikings as raiders was in 793 AD. This was when they raided a monastery in north-eastern England at a place called Lindisfarne. These were Danish Vikings. Danish Vikings would soon control half of England.

For 50 years Vikings raided the eastern shores of England. Then in 865 AD the Danes sent over a Great Army. The Danish King, Guthrum, wanted to make a whole new land for his people.

There were many battles between the people already living in England (the Anglo-Saxons) and the Vikings. Eventually they agreed to share the country. The north-eastern half of England became Viking land, and because the Vikings were Danes, it was called the **Danelaw**.

Did you know… ?

- The Vikings lived in England at the same time as the Anglo-Saxons.
- The Viking age ended in England in 1066, when the Anglo-Saxon king beat off an invasion by the king of Norway.
- Some people call Anglo-Saxon and Viking times the Dark Ages.
- The Danes stopped being pagans when they arrived in England and became Christians.
- Vikings and Anglo-Saxons gradually blended together and were ruled by a single king, who was sometimes of Anglo-Saxon descent and sometimes of Viking descent.

Q **Where did the Vikings first raid in England?**

Viking towns

Most Vikings lived in villages in the country. Very few Vikings lived in towns. The largest Viking town in Britain was York, which the Vikings called Jorvik.

Q Why were planks of wood laid in the streets of Viking towns?

This is a Viking town, with its rows of houses all placed close together. Most people in the town worked at crafts. They had to buy their food from nearby farmers.

Viking towns were small and cramped. They were mainly homes for traders and people making crafts. It was also the place where monks, nobles and even the king lived from time to time.

Did you know... ?

- That Viking villages had their streets paved with wooden slats – so they would not become too muddy in winter.
- Viking towns were places where people could come to settle disputes.
- Jorvik had less than 10,000 people living in it.
- Much of the hard work in a town was done by slaves captured during Viking raids.
- Viking towns were very smelly because many trades such as leather tanning and butchery took place.
- Viking towns would also have been smelly because toilets were just pits dug in the ground with a board on top. When they filled up, someone had to clear the mess out!

The Vikings in North America

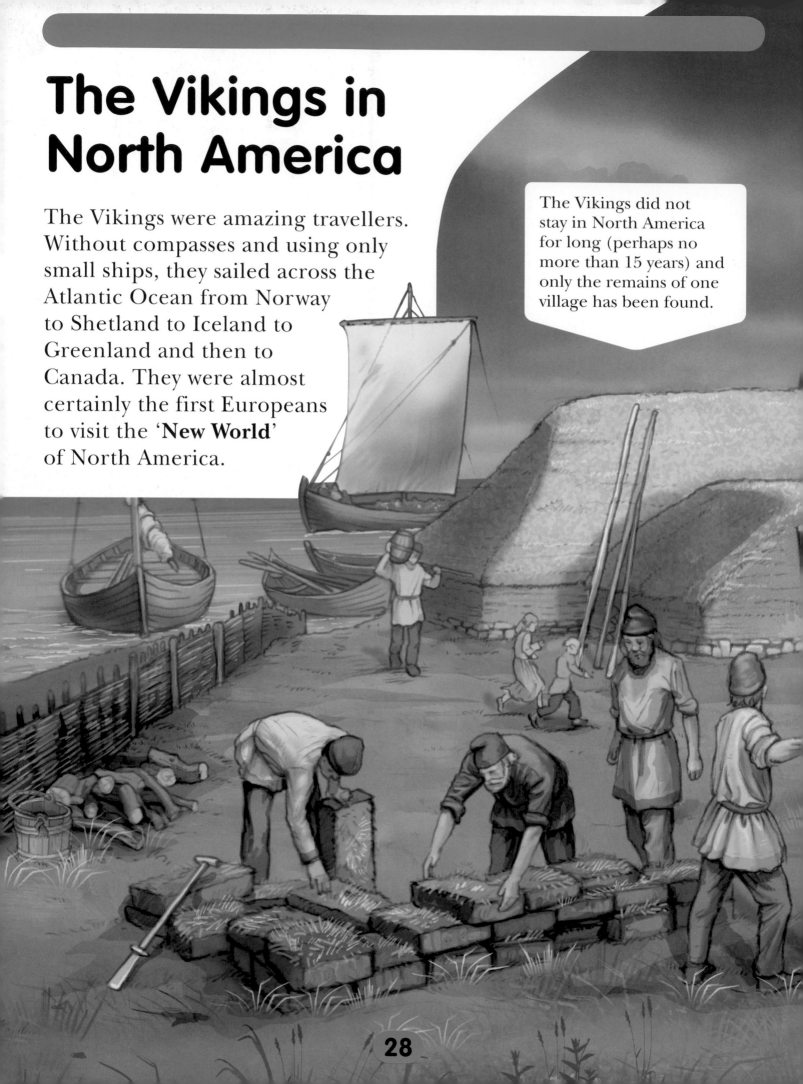

The Vikings were amazing travellers. Without compasses and using only small ships, they sailed across the Atlantic Ocean from Norway to Shetland to Iceland to Greenland and then to Canada. They were almost certainly the first Europeans to visit the '**New World**' of North America.

The Vikings did not stay in North America for long (perhaps no more than 15 years) and only the remains of one village has been found.

Did you know… ?

- The Vikings were probably the first Europeans to reach North America – 500 years earlier than Christopher Columbus!
- The Vikings set up a village in Newfoundland (Canada).
- They probably reached Canada by using Iceland and Greenland as staging posts.
- The Vikings called North America Vinland (Land of Wine) after the wild grapes that were found there.

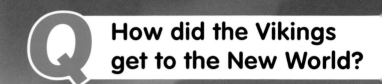

Q How did the Vikings get to the New World?

Try these...

A Viking costume

Make a costume from the items shown in these pictures:

Viking boy

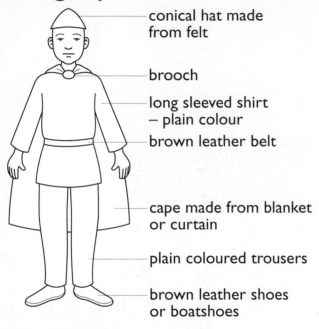

- conical hat made from felt
- brooch
- long sleeved shirt – plain colour
- brown leather belt
- cape made from blanket or curtain
- plain coloured trousers
- brown leather shoes or boatshoes

Viking girl

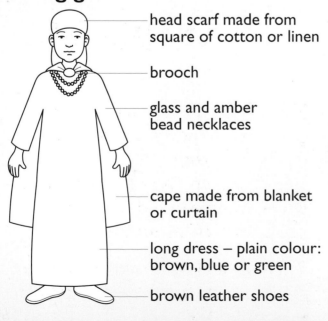

- head scarf made from square of cotton or linen
- brooch
- glass and amber bead necklaces
- cape made from blanket or curtain
- long dress – plain colour: brown, blue or green
- brown leather shoes

Make a Viking brooch

- Draw a design in the oval shape below using a feint dotted line as diagram 1 shows.

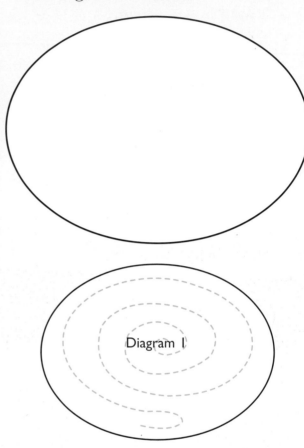

Diagram 1

- Colour in the oval yellow or silvery grey.
- Select a yellow or silvery grey piece of wool and lay it on your design.
- Glue the wool to your design.
- Roughly cut out the oval from this sheet.
- Glue your design to a piece of card.
- Cut out your oval brooch.
- On the other side of the card attach a large safety pin with sticky paper.

Make a Viking sledge

- Cut out the base and sides.
- Bend the sides down so they make a right angle with the base.
- Take two plastic straws with flexible sections and bend up the ends.
- Stick the straws to the sides of the sledge as shown. The straws are the runners of the sledge.
- Cut a piece of straw 10 cm long and stick it to the two bent up ends of the runners. This makes the sledge stronger.
- Devise a test to find the sledge that slides most easily.

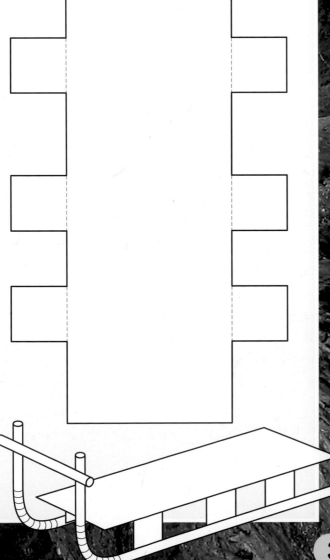

Writing with runes

Here is the original runic alphabet. Notice that one rune may be used for two letters.

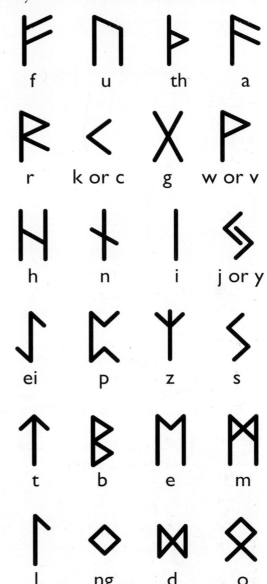

f	u	th	a
r	k or c	g	w or v
h	n	i	j or y
ei	p	z	s
t	b	e	m
l	ng	d	o

Vikings used runes to label their property. In addition to their first name they could have a second name to help identify them. The second name could be about their work or about themselves.

Make a label in runes for an item of your property, such as a pencil case or book.

Glossary

booty The goods the raiding Vikings got in return for taking part in the raid. If the raid was not a success, they got no booty and so went back with no money.

Danelaw The part of England ruled by the Danish Vikings. It was divided up into shires just like the Saxon part.

longhouse A name used for the single room used by Vikings, Saxons and other peoples of this time. In the country the longhouse was used for keeping animals such as cows and sheep in, as well as people. In town a longhouse was a bit shorter as there were no large animals to be housed.

longship A ship that used both a sail and oars.

New World The term Europeans gave to North America simply because, when they discovered it about 500 years ago, it was new to them.

pagan This is a term used to talk about people who believe in a number of superhuman gods who live in a spirit world.

pirate Someone who tries to take the goods of someone else by force.

rune A letter made of straight lines which was part of an alphabet invented by German peoples about 2,000 years ago and used all over northern Europe for nearly 1,000 years.

saga The word saga is Icelandic and means 'a tale'.

Valhalla The hall of those killed in battle. It was the hall looked over by the god Odin. The hall had 540 doors, rafters made from spears and a roof covered with shields.

Index

Curriculum Visions

Curriculum Visions Explorers
This series provides straightforward introductions to key worlds and ideas.

You might also be interested in
Our slightly more detailed book, 'Viking raiders and settlers'. There is a Teacher's Guide to match 'Viking raiders and settlers'. Additional notes in PDF format are also available from the publisher to support 'Exploring Viking times'. All of these products are suitable for KS2.

Dedicated Web Site
Watch movies, see many more pictures and read much more in detail about the Vikings at:

www.curriculumvisions.com
(subscription required)

A CVP Book
Atlantic Europe Publishing © 2007

First reprint 2011.

The right of Brian Knapp to be identified as the author of this work has been asserted by him in accordance with the Copyright, Designs and Patents Act 1988.

Author
Brian Knapp, BSc, PhD

Educational Consultant
JM Smith (former Deputy Head of Wellfield School, Burnley, Lancashire)

Senior Designer
Adele Humphries, BA

Editor
Gillian Gatehouse

Photographs
The Earthscape Picture Library, except *ShutterStock* page 1 (longhouse), 2–3, 30–31.

Illustrations
Mark Stacey except p12 (map), 18–19, 30–31 (diagrams) *David Woodroffe*

Designed and produced by
Atlantic Europe Publishing

Printed in China by
WKT Company Ltd

Exploring Viking times – *Curriculum Visions*
A CIP record for this book is available from the British Library
ISBN 978 1 86214 210 7

This product is manufactured from sustainable managed forests. For every tree cut down at least one more is planted.